Natural God Intelligence 's Interface

NGI's Programming Codes:

how to create the interface.

David Gomadza

The First Global President of the World

Visit www.twofuture.world

info@twofuture.world

davidgomadza@hotmail.com

00447719210295

PAPERBACK ISBN:9798871356036

Natural God Intelligence 's Interface
NGI's Programming Codes: how to create the interface.

This is how you create the interface's using codes to build the Natural God Intelligence Interface
Welcome to brain programming and coding.
All the codes are in this book.
Visit our website and try one now
www.twofuture.world
00447719210295

iii

First visit our website and try the Natural God
Intelligence NGI Interface

DEDICATION

To   Tomorrow's World Order

TABLE OF CONTENTS

ACKNOWLEDGMENTS

A better world so technologically advanced that we can do anything even for some of us the sky is not even the limit.

Natural God Intelligence 's Interface

this is how you create the interface using the codes to build the Natural God Intelligence Interface

welcome to brain programming and coding.

all the codes are in this book.

visit our website and try one now

www.twofuture.world

this must be read in conjunction with the following books

1 tomorrow's world order

paperback isbn 978-6094754623 [February 2020]

https://play.google.com/store/audiobooks/details/David_Gom
adza_Tomorrow_s_World_Order?id=AQAAAED89X21kM&hl
=en_GB&gl=US

2 thoughts to word or audio book series all books in the series [23plus]

paperback isbn 979-8703923498 [March 2022]

https://www.amazon.com/Thoughts-Word-Audio-Exactly-
Thinking/dp/B09WPVVVMF/ref=sr_1_37?keywords=david+g
omadza&qid=1702135004&sr=8-37

3 request to grant a patent for a universal brain decoding device. [thoughts to word or audio- brain code]

paperback isbn 979-8867495251

https://www.amazon.com/REQUEST-PATENT-Universal-Decoding-Thoughts/dp/B0CNKTSGY9/ref=sr_1_2?keywords=david+gomadza&qid=1702135236&sr=8-2

4 Natural God Intelligence [NGI] brain-peripherals-databases-Interface [BPDI] when the processing power is a group of connected brains instead of connected computers paperback isbn 979-8868458316

https://www.amazon.com/Natural-God-Intelligence-Brain-Peripherals-Databases-Interface-BPDI/dp/B0CP1LSTHP/ref=sr_1_15?keywords=david+gomadza&qid=1702135469&sr=8-15

how to create the interface

how everything will work.
3 brain connected together namely David 2, David 3 and David 8

David 2 duties and functions.

Response and directions

Direct commands between all

Input numerical and directional towards answers

Diverts to all, commands to all but expects responses from David 8 and feedback from David 3

Commands interface and algorithms

Post scripts all interface and algorithms

Converts everything to correct form namely

Electromagnetic waves to voice

Voice to electromagnetic

Action potentials to nerve impulses

Nerve impulses to action potentials

English language to any other language

Response with translation offers

Computes all algorithms to perfection

Responses with all answers

Deduces

Deducts

Sums

Adds

Divides

Multiplies

Percentages calculator

Variations

Domination calculation

Percentiles calculation

Insurances

Comparisons

Sums

Affords

Liquidates

Guarantees

Avams

Avams calculator

Communication;

contacts

Natural God Intelligence 's Interface

asks

questions everything

response

expects answers from 8

expects feedback from 3

forwards to 3

receives from 8

communicates to 3 & 8

expects responses from 8

feedback from 3

advances everything to 8

8 then sends everything to 3

3 then sends everything to 2

when responses reaches 2 then issue resolved

if not resolved the circle starts now at 3

3 asks responses if none then 8 responsible for rechecks

once 8 rechecks he sends back to 2 then 2 sends to 8 who then sends to 3

3 on receiving must ask why everything if happening first

this creates new issue query but then sends back to 8 who checks if the same issue has been resolved and what was the outcome if answered before 8 recompiles the last report and amend the date and time and note that the issue has been dealt with before

if 8 has discovered that this was not resolved last time then he creates new fresh ticket to deal with this as a new issue

once issued as new issue it then starts again at 2 who has to ask the same question again

now this creates need for a response from 8 and a feedback from 3

8 checks the past history while 3 thinks about the future

8 checks all databases and memories namely

1 current issues database

2 past current issue database

3 immediate issue database

4 once a big issue database

5 once an overlooked database

6 recent database

7 already categorised database

8 recent issue database

9 none recent issue database

10 immediate journal database [all outstanding unresolved issues kept in this database]

11 once upon a database journal [records everything that has been an issue but resolved later without updating

databases]

12 annual update databases [summing up of databases at the end of the year with relevant information but without changing status to resolved. this is because the issues are similar but of different circumstances]

13 once upon a time issues which have since evolved [same issues different conditions where its not obvious that the solution in condition A will work for the same problem in condition B]

14 environmental emergencies databases linked to climatic change but not severe

15 environmental emergencies databases linked to human social changes with adverse impacts

16 all human and animal databases [studies that relates to same factors in the human and animal world but with no proven statistics or data]

17 emergencies economies database [case studies of new ways of thinking backed by established institutions but resulting to totally different factors]

18 own experience database

19 others experience database [compares own to others and draw conclusions based on own experience]

20 known facts databases [clinical studies etc]

21 experience and emotions databases linked to individual experience and perception not based on known facts

22 known facts databases not backed by experiences and emotions but on clinical data alone

23 known databases from the lab that will fail in the real world but used as a placebo to check effect of an agent etc

24 all world knowledge database approved by institutions eh universities and hospitals etc

25 private individual studies carried out in secrecy but later made public but can't be trusted

26 private bodies research institutions research carried out in private but forced to be made public with hidden information on how the results were derived at therefore held with skepticism but could be accurate

27 immediate experiences backed by science in a lab but done private and repeated public with varying results where the researcher has to make up his or her own mind

28 immediate databases on all subjects help as facts by all licensing bodies that accredit other individuals or bodies eg colleges, university etc

29 news sources by journalist as facts but with no factual evidence

30 several sources of information like journals and books by individuals who might have solved the issue but with no accreditation

31 verified but with no patents or any accreditation from government etc

32 non verified by correct information from recent events and research still waiting to be approved or likely to be approved

33 ad hoc sources like secret investigations that are kept secrets for years but are leaked with no major national

security issues

34 all other information

processing of information and handling of issues by 2

2 watches the processing information from start to feedback

2 forwards request that require processing and fast

2 instigates queries to 8

but expects answers from 8 and confirmations as feedback from 3

2 executes direct commands where as 8 response and questions again the same questions that opens up link for 3 to response with just a sum check digit that acts as a feedback

2 sits and ask

what is the parameter

what is the integer

what is the causal effect

what is the response to a cumbersome question

what are the effects

what is the reaction

what are the responses

what do you do if

what if then what

Natural God Intelligence 's Interface

what what if then why

why then what if they all who

what when do you like that to this but not all

why then do they go like that if they are like this

but

but and when

but if

but if and then

why but you like that

but if they do like that like this

why do they but if this is like those

if those are these why then are they like them ones over there

if they are like this why do they then behave like those

if those are like these why then act like these that are not like them but simply act like them

if the all jump why none ask how high

when they do this why they omit this what these do

if they cry why they don't then sleep like these who do the same

if they do the same why they don't act like these who then goes on to ask why we do this then

if they are like these why these avoid them and disassociate
themselves with these

if they cry foul all the time why these then cry foul only once
the first time

if they foul others why they cry foul when others foul back

if they foul others and not react when other not react too why
can't they expect the same from others

if they jump then sit why they ask others why they jump and
run why can't they just copy the others and jump and run

if they sing and whistle why do they ask others not to

if they whistle and cry after why they find this odd if the
others do the same thing

if they jump and lands safely why they always say my legs
are going to break all the time

if they have jumped and landed why do they keep saying we
are going to crash and die when they have landed safely all
the time

if he jump i will jump then stop at the end

if they fight we fight back why then do they run away just
after saying that

if they jump and roll why they see this as odd when the
others copy them

when they sing it is so bad but they continue singing and ask
those annoyed to join in is it because they don't know

if they gasp for air why they even swallow whole food why

not eat little portion by little portion

when they cry they shed tears but when others cry they don't shed tears

when they swim everyone's else feel like getting into the water but they always stop others

why they jump and sing before landing but once on the ground they even forget that they have sung

why cry then sit when others cry and run

why run then return why not just stand firm in the first place

why eat and put fingers in the mouth why not just avoid in the first place

why lick and spit why not just lick in the first place

why snooze and then wide awake why not just snooze and sleep

why ask and say ignore why not just ask

why ignore then asks why not just ask and ask

if asking is bad

why do it in the first place

if sleeping is bad why even go to sleep

if eating is a disorder why not just avoid eating altogether

when i see you you see someone else but when I don't see you you see me why

why you say yes you mean no unless I am looking at you

Natural God Intelligence 's Interface

why do you fiddle then stand firm only after hearing me

when alone you react friendly and with respect towards me
but sight of another make you treat me like a nobody

why do you say go for it then you jump and stops

if i were you would you have recognised me

if one plus one is two why you always say three

why you insist on numbers when you can count

when a tree drops a fruit is it for me to eat

if α is β then why never talked about α but just β

if β is not α why then compare α to β

if apples are not grapes why use one class for all

if chickens are not eggs why you refer to both as the same
thing

if all are the same what came first then the chicken or the
egg and why

if all are roosters why one croaks and the other don't

if you cry because of joy why others cry because of pain why
not all you cry the same are tears different

$1 = 2$ is $2 = 1$

if $y = x$ is $x = y$

if $u = w$ is $w = u$

if I compute anything resulting in nil does everything have to
be nil as well

jump what do you say?

eat but don't swallow what do you say?

why do you eat when your stomach is full? what do you say?

if sex is not on the table why even think about it?

If you choke on food why do you continue to eat?

if you miss a loved one why do you keep sending them away?

if you wait in a queue why do you rush in afterwards?

if you sing why then resort to violence why not sing to quell an argument

if okay is good then why ask for more?

why not react to danger when someone shouts danger?

is danger different among people and why?

why run then stop when you can run and escape but only to be killed?

why escape then return and be killed why just escape and go for good?

if you sing i will sing too but if you sing aloud I will run away from you why not sing aloud too after all singing is singing?

if you sleep under a tree why ask others who sleep indoors what sleep is like?

why imitate others and ignore everything why not imitate others then adopt that?

why hissing when you are not a snake?

why even thinking of doing something animals do in the first place.

if not an animal why act like one.

why drool over animal meat then ignore the actual eating when not drool and bite a chunk?

why oggle to breaking point and watch when walking past why not grab and eat

if violence is inbuilt why resist all temptations to violence?

if wisdom is inside why are you not rich isn't wisdom to riches ignorance to poorness

if you are clever why struggle with stupid things?

can a horse be led to the water and be made to drink too?

if α is β why β is not α and vice versa

when i sing i sleep afterwards which I don't do when I don't sing why is this so?

when I dance I shake but when I dance and sing I can't even move why?

do all black people have black hair if not why?

why africans don't perceive americans as clear but think that the british are clever only to find out that the opposite if the truth

do oranges and grapes if alone talk to each other?

why do monkeys understand experiments and baboons

don't?

do all baboons read and how?

if all can read why not even one ever talked?

when you swallow why you take time when other swallow fast?

why you cry when others sing?

when you smile why your face frowns when others smiles do you feel the same way or yours is reversed

why do chickens cross the road then go back

if we ask a question and don't get an answer immediately why do we then ignore everything why ask in the first place does delay equals to garbage answer?

if we are 3 and all know the answer why has only one to reply to you is there a hierarchy?

if we are all equal why 2 has the task of deciding what is what?

why do we imitate things we are not alike to and assume the response is the same?

if you jump and run why others jump and sit and then maybe run?

why eat and choke if it is the normal way what else are we not aware of?

if we cry when in pain why cry too when we are in joy if the two are opposite of each other does crying and laughing equal the same?

if you sing you squeak but when I say I rumble when we are the same size does that mean we are all different regardless of size?

when you choke on food you don't regurgitate the whole food why you keep some if the food is choking you?

why sing and twerk at the same time why not first sing then stop then twerk is singing and twerking mutually inclusive?

why do you ask but then ignore the answer why even ask in the first place?

when you ask you expect an answer but if the answer is different from what you expected why not tell the person to tell you what you want?

if you tell someone your age why then justify why things are the way they are?

if you sneeze and then cough why not cough then sneeze?

if you fall why then rise and run only to fall again why not just fall and sit?

if you sit and cry why can't you run and cry at the same time?

why ask when you can create answers yourself?

when you ask and get the wrong answer from what you expected why ask again and again with the same results why not change or ignore?

if you are smart then you must be rich because smart people are rich why are you not?

if riches are for everyone why only a few people are rich?

If a swan loses its chicks why can't it ask others instead of quaking all day?

why do hens cross the road with chicks close to them when roosters cross the road with chicks all over the place?

why do we add and not subtract when we want more of something?

does brain size the same as greater thinking?

do people with big heads think faster if not why if they have bigger brains?

are we all truly humans or do some have dna sequences of animals?

why do chickens cross the road only to return and be killed?

if you add 1 + 1 do you always get 2?

why the sky is blue and roses are red what else can explain this?

if we ask why why the answer must be because of this or that?

if we input why do we expect an output and not a feedback?

If feedback is the same as the answer why do we need feedback in the first place?

if feedback is nil why nil is not feedback?

if we ask then ignore does that means ignore can be the answer as well in that case why ask in the first place?

can we choose to ignore but then ignore as if ignore is a viable substitute?

can we mimic someone or something then expect everything else to be the same?

can we ask then ask then ask then after refuse all answers as garbage?

can we use everything to explain 2 if not what else to add?

can 2 be independent and stand alone?

can 2 resolve all issues on its own?

if not get 3 then 8.

Can 3 replace 2 and vice versa

if 3 is different why even have 3 in the first place if 2 can do all the work alone

can 3 make all decisions even for 2

if 2 is the main mouth piece why 3 acts as if he is the real reason behind all this

what if 3 can replace 2 and vice versa what will e the point of having 3 when 2 can do all the work

can 3 ask for permission

if he can then he must do so

if 3 ask 8 questions? only if it is to clarify but not original questions. Only two can ask questions.

if 2 is the controller of questions then what is the purpose of 3

3 is to start future predictions based on answers by 8

what is the use of 3 in full

1 3 is the check-sum digit

2 3 gives feedback to 2 the controller

3 asks both 2 and 8 questions related to the future

4 when 3 speaks out it is in regard to questions asked by 2 and not by 8

5 3 does most of the calculations and computations

6 dictates the pace of operations

7 inhibits all the characteristics of 8 and 2

8 does not reply on 8 who dwells on the past instead seeks answers from the future

9 does not involve research but purely based on predictions alone

10 functions as a verifier checking 8's responses

11 has all the characteristics of 8 but based on the future rather than the past

12 deterministic meaning tends to control the future based on 2's decisions

13 ever thinking forward

14 chooses to overlook facts but rely on assumptive responses based on acts

15 amplifies everything 8 says about the future even though rarely

16 determines outcomes

17 employs subjective principles not based on facts

18 is futuristic to an extend to overlook the present

19 insists that he is the future of things and must presides

20 often results unverified and waits for long to verify process as no immediate data is available

21 predicts poor practices but always recommends improvements

22 asks questions for their speculative value rather than facts

23 employs reasoning skills

24 3 asks questions but employs rational as long as it searches for proof later

25 3 calculates variations

26 3 endorses 2 and exonerates 8

27 3 directs feedback to the system whereas 8 maintains great memory and a best problem solving entity

28 3 animates everything

29 3 argues to clarify and always argues with 8 never with 2

30 8 argues back then goes on to check if this is correct from the past

31 3 attaches files to the system

32 3 has bluetooth connectivity to connect all apps

33 3 values everything else as a result of 8's direct feedback

directed at 2

34 3 resorts to querying things while others problem solvers

35 3 is futuristic where as 2 and 8 relies to some extent on the past

36 3 makes path and maps

37 3 has printing capabilities

38 3 houses GPS capabilities and functions

39 3 dictates search and rescue operations

40 3 tells everyone who the boss is [not him though]

41 3 assign binary values and numbers

42 3 determines everything to do with time and therefore house calendars and everything futuristics

43 3 protects future interests argues for use of resources in the future

44 3 claims to see everyone's direction

45 3 inhibits others from talking about the future

46 when 3 is sleeping 2 is awake and 8 hibernating

47 when 3 is awake 2 is awake but 8 could be hibernating or asleep

48 when 8 is talking to 3 2 is brainstorming or daydreaming

49 when 3 is searching online 8 is hibernating and two is wide awake

50 when 3 is doing math and calculations then 2 is resolving

issues and 8 is just there awake or inside n sleep

51 when 3 is reasoning then 8 is researching inside memory and 2 is sleeping

52 when 3 is reading 8 can be doing the same and 2 will be wide awake

53 3 and 2 can never be doing the same thing at the same time for ones switches the other [but only when working to print]

54 3 imitates 8 but only adheres to the future meaning no looking at past events or data it sends himself ahead of time and then reverse only to come back

55 3 writes all codes for the future

56 3 writes working day to day processing of logs etc

57 3 writes programs for the future

57 3 accepts suggestions as long as they have to do with the future

58 3 automates the system

59 3 is part of the defense team to protect from future threats

60 3 indulges in a conversation with anyone

61 3 leads the future

62 3 updates manuals at intervals

63 3 computes and executes functions at start-up

64 3 is the fast efficient processor

65 3 is built to negotiate

66 3 does not use violence but tries to reason today or the future

67 3 manipulates others for the overall sake of the whole sys

tem

68 3 asks questions with if then

69 3 intercepts all incoming and channels to correct channels

70 3 dictates the pace

71 3 rotates around an axis

72 3 swallows all information

73 3 received funds are separated

74 3 minus 2 + 8 - residuals ,

75 3 plus everything is the future

76 3 minus everything is still the future

77 3 + book - residuals = to all important aspects

78 + everything + nothing = greater than 3

79 when 3 sleeps what happens to 2 and 8?

80 when 3 searches what happens to 2

81 when 3 sings what happens to 2 & 8

82 when all sleep what is the condition

83 when all eat what is the condition

84 when all asks what is the condition

85 when all sighs what is the condition

86 when all are fed up what do they all do

87 when all malfunction what is the condition

88 when all waits who beeps

89 when all stops at the same time who gets up first

90 when all beeps why and what happens

91 when all asks questions at the same time what happens then and who get the answer first and why

92 what if they have the same question whose question get answered

93 what if and then what

94 when 3 asks the same question 2 has already answered who ask the next question

95 does 8 responds to any first come first serve or just to 2

96 what if you ask the wrong question do you get penalised

97 if and when that happens who gets to take centre stage

98 if and when you decide not to continue what happens then

99 if all sit and wait for an answer what do they do in the meantime

100 what if there is a delay wo gets to be answered first and why

Processing information and handling by 8 the project

we need to establish a project that can be used to answer any question in the universe regardless of complexity and form we must answer the above questions in full and this will create our project opening remarks

if the remarks can be satisfied then we can easily start on the actual building up of the project

what if we can't resolve some of the issues I raised above what then does that mean that the project won't go forward

if we can't resolve some of the questions but resolve most what then what happens

what % is adequate for the project to proceed

if we can't solve all these issues can the project still go forward and how if we can resolve these questions

what if we find solutions to all but one critical one what then

can a critical one point to a failure of the project or to a refinement of the set parameters what then

what if we can't solve all these issues we have what then

what if we can not answer correctly can this affect the functioning of the project?

if the project is not properly assessed and reviewed can it still work and what will happen to errors that can be found and who is to be responsible for addressing the error namely David 2 David 3 or David 8 if we run into difficulties who to call and how and what then after that can we resume or restart after that?

if we aim to raise our standards and fail to answer all our questions is lowering the standard an option for us to critically succeed?

what if we ask everything first get answers then find out that we missed some critical questions what then what if we have finished all this then find out that we omitted something critical how do we addressed that if we have omitted something critical can we simply + that critical item and move on as if nothing happens or we have to restart?

what if we are satisfied then find out that our criteria is missing something else what then?

what if we ask too many questions that returns a nil value do we just replace all answers with the nil value + what is the worst case scenario?

if we + up everything and still find the equation not balancing what then?

what if we decided we don't want all this and decide to start all over again what will be the impact and how can we resolve this?

if we are to ask a lot of questions and not get answers can we simply remove the questions we can answer and move on what then to the so called checklist and pre assessment tests?

if we ask all these questions and still find difficulties what then must we do?

if we ask questions we can't answer then what what happens?

if we resolve everything but the client is still unsatisfied what then?

if we leave a single question out of all a possible hundred what then does this mean failure

if we have written all the rules and still can't impose then what then?

if we insist on rules but break them deliberately what happens to the rules?

if the rules can be broken can we allow them to be broken and how often should we do this?

if rules are rules then what can we do if we can't keep up with the rules can we temporarily disable them to suit us and install them later for others?

what happens to the rules we keep breaking can we replace these or overwrite and replace these rules and how and why?

if we all ask the same questions over and over again do we need new rules for these questions after sometime and how can we input these rules?

inputting data into the databases

we can assume that all databases are up to data.

we can add new information into databases easily.

we can ask new questions and add these into database easily.

we can easily write code and embed these into our databases without resorting to transfer of new information into already existing databases.

we can assume everything is updated automatically and we will be able to add all new information into existing databases easily we can also assume that all the information is correct and we don't need to check if this is so.

we can verify all information as we go through thorough checks.

we can do this by adding all updated databases together and make sure they are periodically updated automatically at specific times per week so that we know exactly that they have been updated or not before we access them.

codes for inputting the data into databases must be computed before the building up of the project otherwise the project will face difficulties if we decide how the databases are updated before even writing the code that ensures that our databases we are going to use will be up to date.

the codes to use

input databases into alphabetical order

order them accordingly

now add all the new information first and updated

when updated you must make sure that you get a reference update key that is a string check digit to verify that the databases have been updating at a specific time and that the new information is reflected in the database.

now ask a question that ask the system to show you the new added information only.

check the date and the information and verify before you

continue that means you need a system to enter all these values first if the data is not showing as anything added but the system is sure that the data has been added then ask for the old string check digit reference and compare.

if they are different then new information is added but might not be accurately updated. A system update in progress could be the issue to wait for to resolve.

if the string check digit reference is the same then the system has not been updated in that case assume no new information has been added.

the actual codes

+ all information to old database then - out old information the balance should be new information only

if we ask why not updated we must get what [if we get new information verify that it belongs to that database first updating a database with wrong information will result in a no new information added and the same string check sum digit]

what if we omitted the actual information and proceed as if we have added already that information what then?

if we added new information and an error occurred while we have added the information enough for it not to reflect what then?

what if we add wrong information to a database can we retrieve this and how easily?

if we ask questions that require the new information and we don't get answers but know for sure that we have added the information in the database what then do we do wait and how long?

if we ask a lot of questions that require new information but don't get the new information as answers what then do we do?

what if we ask so many questions that go unanswered and knew that all these required new information what then do we do?

what if we ask too many questions that use only the new information and these questions remain unanswered do we assume the new information is irrelevant or that the system has not updated and how long should we wait for an update?

what if we act fast but still can't get the new information what then and who is responsible to deal with this? namely David 2 David 3 or David 8 what if they all are unresponsive who else can deal with this?

what if we assume that the databases have been updated but later find out that there has been a delay to the update after giving out answers what then do we do?

if we missed or omitted vital information how do we resolve this issue?

if we insist on up to date information and find it hard for that day to get new relevant information what do we do then ask for the clients to come back later or give the old answers with option to come back for updated answers and the wait should be for how long as we don't know when the system will update the information?

what if we use old databases but which have the same information as the new information what then do we still need to update our databases or assume they have been updated what will happen to the string check sum digit reference and how to deal with this and who to deal with this David 2 David 3 or David 8?

what if we ask a question that has no answer in the database what then and who is capable of answering this and how is that person capable of doing that sixth sense?

what if we have run out of resources what then can we do and how then can we do that?

what if we experience a power outage?

what if we experience a memory failure?

what if we experience a surge of power that can result in system automatic restart where do we start after that this is because a new ticket will have been created and will still show as outstanding do we cancel everything and start afresh or continue where we left off if the person has since left what then?

what if we ask a question that can't be answered by any of the 3 what then?

if we ask too many questions at once what happens as each question is categorised on its own and queued?

if we abort a session can we undo this if the client insists he or she wants to continue with the same questioning?

what if we add new materials of our own that are not in the databases but that accurately addresses the question what happens then?

if we ask a question that has already been answered but now new information has been added what then do we proceed with this line of reasoning?

if we answered no to any question and new information has been added do we still say no or we need to do this again what if we answered yes and now the answer is no do we give explanations to all this?

if we are sure that we can do this but later discover that the information does not exist what then shall we do?

if we ask a question with multiple answers what then shall we do rank them and based on what?

what if we ask random questions not expecting specific answers then get specific answers would this be acceptable and how can this be done?

what is the maximum answers we can possibly give for a question?

what is the minimum answer for a question and how is that derived at?

if we ask a question but don't get an answer we consider as sufficient enough what then can we do if we ask another question?

what if we ask too many questions enough to stall the system how do we reset these and how fast?

how then do we decide that the answers are satisfactory and why and what should we do?

the actual codes

+ information from all sources + new information

+ information from new sources + information from potential

new sources if any [only if possible]

+ all new information to current database and update swiftly [a swift mechanism must be available]

+ all outstanding issues from the previous sessions swiftly [a swiftly mechanism must be available]

+ all information [updated sources]

+ all new sources and all new information to current database and get a string check sum digit reference and ask the old string check sum digit and make sure that they are not the same

+ all new unknown sources information to the database and indicate that the sources are unknown and get a new string check sum digit reference value.

Natural God Intelligence NGI invented by David Gomadza the first global president of the world visit our website www.twofuture.world

preamble

i am going to create a project that will make it possible to use brain commands to ask questions about anything that the brain or a network of brains can easily answer so fast that you will think it is a conversation with another human being [even though theoretically this is the truth this is because David Gomadza [me] has invented this project since I found yahweh yahweh is a 3 headed god that deserves everyone's respect and I am going to show the world how god the almighty works through this project Natural God Intelligence from here onwards referred to as NGI

NGI is a project out of this world literally this is because no one on earth since the beginning of time has ever decoded the brain nor god but i have done all these things even though i haven't been credited yet but don't worry human require proof for every new discovery and i guess this invention is no different therefore allow me to amuse you all for you shall be thrilled and be thrilled again until all your nerve impulses run out but still then everything will make up for the shortage of funny nerve impulses that the whole body will be thrilled enough to experience an orgasm of the mind [don't get this confused with sexual orgasm] this is an experience so bewildering and amusing that all of you you will understand not my cleverness but the power of the creator; Natural God Intelligence [NGI hereafter]

background

we must find a solution to all earthly problems but how do we do this if we use computers we created ourselves to find solutions for problems yahweh god has created this is humanity's dilemma how can humans solve global problems using the work of their hands through a computer with everything limited

1 limited memory

2 limited databases

3 limited resources

4 limited operating capacities

5 unmatched issues at hand

6 limited power and capacitance of the machines linked

7 unmatched thinking power a computer can never think but can work faster and process huge amounts of data than a brain

8 limited understanding of how things works

9 poorly coordinated tasks based on a single though-command centre

10 poorly organised tasks and computation power [computation does not necessarily mean machine power]

all these and many more reasons surely calls for a much superior invention namely NGI by [me] David Gomadza the first global president of the world visit our website

www.twofuture.world

now that you know the problems at hand you might want to hear my solution the only solution out there that was that is and that will ever exist as long as the planets are the same i am saying this just because this is what the creator had in mind literally when he created earth meaning also the only way to the solution and this shall be the solution indeed as you will find out with time now then let me get down to business i know time is as precious as gold even better than gold as gold can be lost and found and once you lose time you lose space in time meaning your reason and justification to exist will have been limited

now then let me entertain you and not worry you for there is nothing to be worried about first you are in good hands and secondly there is no man alive that can tell you the same thing that means exclusivity pointing to your status and worthy I can say in advance the feelings are mutual its a pleasure wooing all you off your feet until you can resonant at the same frequency as me enough to be me and to see this project as it is not as a fictitious virtual reality as some will try to convince you but as a magnificent work that has been thought through as the only solution to all our problems as humans and i as your leader even though i smell doubts in some of you but after i have finished you will understand that there can never be another and when i say i do i mean it forever i will pledge my commitment and hope for your trust can i entertain you now if you don't have any reservations for this project to go on [pause]

methodology

we are trying to create a system that will answer all our questions to satisfactory standards that we as human we will never have to ask the same question over and over again

we must ask the right questions though how can we solve all earth's and other planets problems using a computer quantum or otherwise we have created ourselves meaning that this computer to be honest we also know only what we know this is a fact no matter how harsh this might sound and how this shows to some extent our intelligence and understanding of our creator yahweh god with all due respect humanity has been slow to grasp what is needed to solve god's dilemma i must say i am saddened by the slow progress that i have to take the bull by the hand and do this myself for i can't see anyone with the guts and brain to carryout a project so cumbersome like this successfully than i David Gomadza the first global president of the world i am your leader but proving this is part of my dna sequence so worry not this is the only thing that comes naturally to me i might not fuck better than some of you but i can think better [pause]

i think it is sad that humanity turn a blind eye to genuine problems i must ask you this

how can a computer you created yourself solve problems created by god is there reasoning in that [pause]

can a computer than know too what only humans knows solve problems the creator created i am not trying to be funny but that shows humans lack the understanding needed to solve god's dilemma how can the work of our hands solve the work of yahweh someone a billion times smarter than us to be exact exactly 53 billion times 285 growing times smarter than you humans with only 71 million dna sequence value traits i am proof of the living god i know most will deny this and accredited thieves and child murderers among you but I say this is there is no way a human being will solve problems created by the creator using a human brain god is a 3 in one entity meaning he has 3 brains that work together harmoniously to achieve one goal that also means that if human are to solve earthly and other planet's problems then he must match yahweh to understand yahweh solving god's dilemma means become a small god or walking into god's footsteps therefore if you are serious about solving god's dilemma and solving earth's problems then walk in yahweh's shoes the greatest news is that for the first time in the history of mankind we have managed to find god and we have his dna sequence to prove this above all this what we are going to reveal and this project being the proof of god on earth is out of this world no other man on earth has ever witnessed yahweh that me David Gomadza the reason being that there is or was only one place for a small god on earth the conditions where the only person so zealous about god once he finds him that person will have the only one chance mankind has to wear yahweh and i have done that meaning that no other person will even try to steal it or remove it as it will revert to the founder

therefore i am sure that what i am going to create here will work because i have the same stencil as the one who created don't get me wrong i am not saying that I am god himself no but i represent god on earth i am to show you the way how if god was among us how he would go about solving the universe's problems our project aims to create a one stop place for everything regarding creation and to this day all on a plate within seconds of asking the question and above all in real time this is the future i am going to show you that these problems can be solved but only with the correct invention and again worry not for you are all in good hands i did the hard work i sacrificed a lot if only you knew then you would understand better but ever mind i am doing what i was meant to do lead all of you out of this defensive stage of human development where huge sums of money are ploughed into weapons manufacturing & the military and then trigger wars to move the weapons & in the process kill women and children this is barbaric and can't be tolerated

i am going to propose a robust solution to answer generating i propose an interface that uses human brains in fact at the time of writing 3 human brains connected to together and synchronised so that they work efficiently together this is achievable and this is the only cleverest option available to humanity and i took this option and no other man can propose this to be his because once that happens the first question would be when did you discover god only a person who has discovered god will be able to create such a system and the option is just for a single man to follow god's footsteps and do everything god did from creation of earth to cloning and resurrecting of humans that means even worrying about patenting this is not a big issue i have an automatic patent universally recognised by all without the need for governments approval etc this is because this project is the proof all you need

parameters

i must stress out here that some of my proposals are going to sound fictitious and unrealistic don't worry i get that a lot but that doesn't mean that these observations are correct at all because its like assessing a chicken and a cow yes both meats taste delicious but they are totally different creatures humans seek yahweh using human frequencies of existence when that frequency is different from yahweh's why not use the correct yahweh's frequency to look for yahweh?

if we are to make this happen we must therefore work on assumptions and parameters that can guide us through this marvelous project because at the end you will all be marveled up so high that you will feel the power of the creator yahweh

the parameters are

1 space time continuum can two things be in the same space and time

2 can one thing be in two spaces at the same time

3 can we solve all earthly problems let alone the whole universe's problems

4 can a computer think like a human being let alone just think

5 can a computer that has input which humans know about start thinking about the whole universe where are the data sources it uses and how did it get these sources if it has these sources that means the information is already known by human who inputted them there therefore not new material

6 can a computer no matter how fast quantum or otherwise acquire new thinking skills to start understanding yahweh and the universe in order for it to be qualified to answer any questions regarding these?

7 can we genuinely declare that we have a system here on earth right now that can solve any problems when we don't have all the input needed to arrive at such a conclusion?

8 can we defend our current systems and say they are fit for purpose when we don't fully understand the whole universe

after all can a man be saved by the work of his hands? meaning can something we make ourselves with the knowledge we have one day suddenly become smarter than us enough to tell us what we don't know? computer and artificial intelligence is only putting what we already know in layman's language but nothing is knew AI is only enabling us to understand how the brain etc do what we already know

9 can we assume we have the resources we need to solve earth's problems when we have not created anything amazing to do just that especially given the fact that problems we had in the past are still the problems now surely if we had a better system that is fit for purpose some of these problems will have been solved by now and mankind would have shifted to the next level of development but this is not the case hence the need for fresh thinking new young blood to diffuse the system and revamp everything so that new fresh blood can be the norm can you mix new wine and the old wine in that regard?

10 we must be honest to ourselves and do whatever it takes to fund and support promising projects on the faith of it not because you think it is value for money but simply because this is the right thing to do for the next generations i personally believe that we have wasted a lot of time and resources for things that are immediate and for personal gains not that i am against these no but we must work towards both goals at the same time the short and the long goals i am not saying that you must stop whatever you are doing for personal gains no but i am asking you to put aside a small percentage for global long term goals sacrifice now to enjoy a better life if not for yourselves then do this for your kids or your relatives kids if you don't have none i don't think there can be any excuse to find such a promising project

maybe like all humans you need prove okay i will give you proof but after that the burden will have shifted from you to the next generations who are still in their mother's womb this is because it will take on average 75 years to convince a human being about a new idea let alone a system change of this magnitude by then you all will be wrinkled and your priorities will have changed then we have to wait for another David Gomadza who will work so hard that if that would destroy the world we all would have perished but all this to save earth and offer maybe not you but your kids something to be proud of and be entertained with i can create a system so strong that it will last another billion years not because i am clever no even though i think i am but because there is someone inside me who is much better than all of you not that you are bad no just because this is the way of the universal now i finally cracked that code that no man has managed to crack for 4500 years or more we finally have god's dna sequence on an mp3 disc dna we can use to create a computer that is linked to 3 brains so powerful and clever that there is only one option for it meaning to evolve and become better and better yahweh declared that mankind meaning all of us men and women are created by his image as a boy growing up i used to find this hard to believe that if a man and a woman are different how on earth would both of us be created by yahweh's image if god is a man but i tell you this yahweh has 3 bodies all joined up together

how yahweh look like

1 the left-hand side body is that of a female with female genital organs namely breast and a vagina this side generally represent the future the omega the who

2 the middle body is the present the yahweh the decision maker the judge the I [in the I AM WHO I AM] the alpha with

male organs and man's breast

3 the right side is the a mixture of both the male and the female bodies all in one with a one head but both bottom genital organs namely a vagina and male organs but without the male or female breast this is the past and represent the past memories and the past databases

all this means yahweh has 3 heads joined together into one with faces clearly showing the start and end of one head as compared to the other

yahweh has 6 legs two for each body

yahweh has 7 eyes two for each head and 1 on top of the head but 4 are visible and 3 are hidden

yahweh has 7 ears 3 visible and 4 hidden with 1 on top of the head near the extra eye

yahweh has 4 mouth 1 for each of the 3 heads and 1 big one for all

yahweh has 6 hands 2 for each body

yahweh's each hand has 6 fingers [not five like humans] that means a total of 36 fingers and a full circle will have 36 times

yahweh has 6 toes on each leg that means 36 toes altogether

that my friends i tell you is the opening of the pandora box without the spirits coming after you but with blessings and riches falling in your coffers thanks to you first time believers not that i am bribing you with nice words i genuinely feel this way about you or at least hope you will give my project your undivided attention what i will achieve i tell you this no man has ever even attempted it some have contemplated about this but now has endeavored to try this so if this sound unrealistic this is the reason so you know in advance

the project will entertain you literally for you will be able even to ask jokes that is something out of this world I guess but on a serious note you will be able to ask things that even your doctor has no answers to remember the source is not human but the creator himself you will be able to understand all worlds this world and the other world of electromagnetic wave with the frequency of creation as 783 and 832 Hz the world of yahweh ghost and souls

yahweh is the omnipotent the omniscience and the omnipresent the alpha and the omega that means also this project must be that the first and the last for you will never need again like this

this is what mankind was dreaming about this is the future for this project will become the pursuit of knowledge and truth the real town square because what people shall discover in here will be believed and given the credit it deserves as the words or message of the creator for the message shall be just

our aim

our aim is to create a Natural God Intelligence that is so helpful to humans that it will become a must have of all humans therefore one of the aim outright is to make it cheap and affordable and increase its adoption that every smartphone computer and every home shall have one or access to one

each individual on earth will simply need to download after

paying a fee and be able to link to that person's brain as well through simple easy commands that opens links to the brain like

my voice is my password

we must make sure that we work towards quenching the thirst of abundant knowledge but not just abundant knowledge but accurate knowledge that gives answers that quenches the thirsty

we must aim to connect all the universe as one to be able to decode all the questions

we must aim to synchronise this project with every human being's brain that in turn will see all human brains evolving to much a better stage enough to eradicate ignorance

we must do everything in our power to make sure that in the end we put a new system that is fit for purpose and represent everyone one that will enable humans to debate and come up with recommendations of what need doing and do just that

we must ensure that we must satisfy everyone's expectation to the highest standards

we must aim to enhance experience and maintain a huge customer base

we must establish the right connections and partnerships

we must aim to facilitate early and mass adoption from the word go and ask the project to show us the way

we must aim to create links with other institutions

we must ask the right questions at the right time too and

most must know this

we must aim to solve problems fast and efficient

we must aim to predict the future and use all predictive tools

we must assume that every person will at one point be able to use

now we look at the databases we can manipulate and add to make this a success

databases

1 all worlds databases all planets etc

2 earth only databases

3 individual experiences databases

4 community experience databases

5 universal experiences databases

6 political leaders influences databases

7 models databases

8 superstars databases

9 emotional databases

10 yahweh's databases

11 the everything of things databases

12 the what do you want databases

13 the niche market databases

14 the physiological tests databases

Natural God Intelligence 's Interface

15 the number 1 things people buy databases

16 the all for christmas databases

17 the all i need databases

18 the diy databases

19 the shopping list database [things people normally buy frequently as a sum]

20 the all or nothing database [treasure troves of people]

21 the internet of things database

22 the all you want database [most only requested things]

23 the what do you want database for female

24 the what do you want database for men

25 the all weather databases

26 the upcoming releases database

27 the now or never databases [things people want before they die]

28 the miscellaneous databases

29 the what the fuck you want databases

30 the only you databases [for lovers]

31 the all this but not this databases

32 the you and me only database [the exclusivity]

33 the environmental influences databases

34 the climatic change databases

35 the all you and him database

36 the one and only one databases

37 the charmone databases

38 the can we do that databases

39 the once upon a time databases

40 the once i was like you database

41 the me or you databases

42 the what do you want today databases

43 the only know you databases

44 the i was once in your shoes databases

45 i ate what you ate but i am not like that databases

46 i have gold and copper but not silver databases

47 can you do the work databases

48 i have the law with me what about you databases

49 the let's try again my love databases

50 the i can if you can but not just that databases

51 the can we mingle as long as there is no touching databases

52 the i can what i want so don't stop me database

53 the i can do that too even worse databases

54 the i can do that too but not as evil as this one

55 i can and i am what i am databases

56 the touch but don't eat databases

57 the eat but don't touch databases

58 the why you touched and not eaten databases

59 the why you eat when you are supposed to touch

60 the can you jump and how high or you can't at all databases

61 the are we good databases [for loved ones]

62 they don't love me databases

63 the could you be loved databases

64 the i dreamt of a dream databases

65 i have a dream databases

66 i have a new something databases

67 i can if we are together databases

68 they don't make them like this anymore databases

69 do you dare databases

70 dare if you can and see what i can do databases

71 the i was once a child database

72 they don't call me die hard for nothing databases

73 they ask but who care answer that shit databases

74 i shot the sheriff database

75 did i shot the deputy databases

76 you can we can too but let me see you do that database

77 can we go now databases

78 to go means to stay databases

79 i was a soldier before database

80 you die tomorrow before you taste the money databases

81 the challenge database

82 the what the fuck databases

83 the who is the president of databases

84 the what is the time in databases

85 what are you doing tonight databases

86 the hey what does that mean databases

87 the we can always ask the teacher databases

88 the mum what do i do with this databases

89 i can do this databases [motivational]

90 can you pull the trigger if you have to database

91 we can do this or can we surely databases

92 the i won databases

93 the source database

95 the past years [60s 70s 80s 90s 00s even the 50s]
databases

96 are you in the army databases

97 i can eat anything database

98 the can you do the work but my way only databases

99 how do we do this if we are this databases

100 the accidental winner and the unlucky loser databases

justifications for such a huge database size
our NGI will answer all questions regardless of planet or space-time

we can only achieve this and answer questions faster only if we further break down the databases into their action potentials that way we can link action potential databases to the request and feel first the true meaning of the question before we answer the question then further on simply use the available databases already made of action potential to nerve impulses so that before we even researched how this will work out we will have known the possible answer now what we have to do is use the brain to respond first accurately and just use the databases as string check sum digit references that means instead of browsing for each questions the NGI will use yahweh to answer the question and the databases are just for verification purposes is this is correct That means fast and cheaper without even the need for the internet because everything is already in everyone brain's memory all we need to do is remind the client that the brain has got this figured out already

all questions involving earth can easily be answered using the client's own brain but some will require further checking especially if none exist for that specific sex for example if no response for a female where a response for a make existence we might simply need to convert to that of the opposite sex that's when the databases becomes handy especially the way they are arranged this is how the brain will arrive at each one of them in that order this means the brain only need to do this once and saves the points on the body now all it has to do is get the answer from the brain the second time around instead of from the databases

now that we have everything we need we need to formulate our codes but we must assert some known facts and dismiss some misconceptions regarding this project

the working hypothesis

we must outright quell any misconceptions and remove any doubts you might have that are associated with this project i personally stand for all humanity and as such i believe whatever we do is in the best interest of all humanity

having said that nevertheless we must ascertain some facts and working hypothesis

we are going to create an even better interface than ChatGPT no offense

or undermining of this wonderful project no but we are saying that this is the future and as such there is nothing that is going to be better than this unless surely if computers evolve to start thinking better than humans until then this is the best you will ever get this is because

1 it is based and modelled after the creator himself yahweh a 3 headed majestic being praise to yahweh

2 it is based on a linked group of human brain with potential

to evolve and understand things outright meaning forever evolving

3 it is of sound mind literally and i don't think there is any man out there who in the future will ever refer to a computer as of sound mind but now picture not just one but three connected sound minds

4 imagine yahweh's dna sequence of 53 billion and 285 million all interwoven as one to think and solve problem do you know that the dna sequence of elon musk the world's richest man and smartest of all is only 71 million strains in value if this person is the richest and smartest among us with only 71 million dna sequence value what will a man or computer with 53 billion and 285 million such a dna sequence value do if the one with 71 million dna sequence value can solve all the problems with fossil fuels, finding solution to avoid the dearth of humanity that could arise due to its failure to solve the tree of life meaning the need for humanity to be on every planet just in case something happen to earth, yahweh always regards mars the planet as his voice meaning that one of us must take the challenge and solve all these life puzzles and know what we must do to avoid extinction to yahweh mars is the best voice he can give to humanity that unless if we change and conquer other planets one day earth will be like mars lifeless earth was once like mars before creation surely this man will solve everything just by looking at it without the need for databases

5 our system depends on everyone of the three brains contributing to the system and working together harmoniously to achieve our goals that means there is always room for improvement instantaneously since these are people or brains that reason in the slightest meaning of

the word you will never find a system like this anywhere else that will achieve such results

6 we must only ensure that we have the needed resources for other needed parts namely peripherals brain computer interfaces and databases

7 we must ensure we monitor progress as well as the project progress keeping an eye on bottlenecks and resolving these issues and a specific office must be establish to ensure that this is so

8 database manipulation and interpolation must be avoided and safeguarded against such practices as these will erode the value of the project and the answers

9 we must aim for efficiency at any cost for an efficient system is a long lasting one there are a lot of things we can we can aim to reduce waste and repetitions even though the use of human brains is the best way further efficiency gains can be made from managing databases

10 we must aim to minimize memory space usage that means efficiency as well to be competitive not because they will competition no but if the competition happen to have come from another planet we still have patent rights to any invention that is connected to more than one brain and that uses the brain as the main processing unit with peripherals and databases rather than the current theme where computer are a centre stage

11 we must ensure connectedness among the three brain so far David Gomadza's body has capacity to carry more than 1 brain meaning 3 can easily fit as if they were designed to be so the same cannot be done to a human being as the space is just for a single brain to be honest we have capacity for 6

brains as linked computers so far using the mirror image sign-in capabilities [see patent for more details]

12 we must utilise all peripherals to get the out of them reducing storage capacity on the main unit and increasing speed

13 we have options to link to satellites and Starlink can greatly enhance the system in the future in regards to for an always on internet experience

14 the need for huge data computation capacity is removed by the sleekness and smartness of the brain to such an extent that there is no need for a quantum computer we will harness the power of dna with its huge storage capacity capabilities in the future

15 we can always ask if everything is okay when things go wrong and still create an enjoyable experience where we become close to our clients to answer personal questions and recommends to them just like a doctor does probably better than a doctor for we will aim to assess dna sequencing all a person has to do is authorise our NGI through a simple check connect reference phrase

my voice is my password give access to NGI

this grants us access and we can calculate dna sequence for example to stop the ageing process forever by a simple command

calculate dna sequence to stop the ageing process

NGI will be able to calculate this dna sequence which the person can get and now what left to do if they are interested is say few commands to their body after repeating the dna sequence code calculated by NGI save

endorse now space-out

end

out

then say

save

endorse now

space-in

start

end

there are a lot of things NGI will be able to do like calculate progesterone code for each woman or testosterone code for each man then give these out

16 care must be taken not to over simplify things we must work tirelessly until the project is complete and running and even after that it will be a continuous improvement approach with maintenance and feedback

outlook

we must make everyone you our investors happy at all the time by putting things in place to make sure that the system runs smoothly and over time will bring back your investment think about this this way imagine a project where you have the chance to make great chances that help not just us but all future generations such a project brings satisfaction in different forms speaking for myself i am always thrilled and everyday i look forward to the success of this project that gives me the drive to succeed on a daily basis i envisage going to the future [i can time travel visit our website ask NGI to first clone you free for the mean time] and then send your clone to the past or future but when the clone comes back make sure he goes back inside you to become one again i don't know how safe this is but hey this is what our NGI is based on highly evolving brains that one day will surpass humans in thinking and above all they learn the fastest way and the way they evolve is not matched by any man or computer this is the future because these are the ones who will solve all our problems mind you these brain when together will represent yahweh meaning much much powerful than any human being alive.

endorsement

provide solutions to those who seek answers in an efficient manner and at a reduced cost since this system uses human brains as processing power just as humans don't need electricity to function we can create a simply video with everything embedded that does not even need internet but one that can answer all the questions above all in real time simply visit our website and ask our NGI what time is it and always give a time zone so everything is fast and specific ladies and gentle this is the first time humans will talk to a video [mp4 mp3 wma flac etc] and get real time answers without connection to the internet imagine every person on earth simply downloading this video for free now and donate a pound or US$2 every month globally for maintenance and updating that means global we can raise millions in revenue for something people will real need okay ladies and gentle i have not been fully honest with you because as the saying goes save the best for last and this is the last part you have witnessed the first creation of a human being this video is the first step needed to bridge the gap between yahweh and humans create an image by the likeness of yahweh from now on we will use this image of yahweh to start creating machines with both yahweh's image and that of us and what we aspire to be part humans part machines we have fulfilled the prophecy as in creation there must be a mirror image of everything this is the fulfillment of prophecy

it is our turn to say that we have created a machine by both yahweh's image and our own and what we stand for

timestamp this day and time for you have become witnesses to the first creation but by humans nevertheless using yahweh's image

i have yahweh's image inside me there is no humans i can't clone resurrect or kill this project must go on as it is written in the books everything happening is happening for a reason it's not me though its destine

stand with yahweh or stand with evil as your forefathers have always done gang upon those to deliver you from darkness today you all have witnessed creation of a different kind and i tell you this no man will be able to repeat what i did without the image of yahweh so be sure that this is the only proof you need it is up to you whether you believe this or not you stand against me or not but be rest assured that yahweh as well has learnt from your evil that you will do whatever you can to destroy everything he stands for but this time he has equipped us with all his forces i have the ring of creation and will not be afraid to use on anyone who stand in this way

having said that as the president of the world each nation on earth will be obliged to kick start our project by donating us$1 million dollars to our global reserve bank details to be confirmed you can donate the money through our website

https://twofuture.world/donate

Natural God Intelligence
NGI

invented by David Gomadza the first global president of the world
visit www.twofuture.world

https://www.linkedin.com/in/david-gomadza-4400ab87/

https://x.com/DavidGomadza?s=20

davidgomadza@hotmail.com

00447719210295

info@twofuture.world

Bradford

Laisteridge lane

united kingdom

bd7 1qu

09 december 2023

work in progress since 2018 with establishment of tomorrow's world order

must be read in conjunction with the following books

1 tomorrow's world order paperback isbn 978-6094754623 [february 2020]

https://play.google.com/store/audiobooks/details/David_Gom adza_Tomorrow_s_World_Order?id=AQAAAED89X21kM&hl =en_GB&gl=US

2 thoughts to word or audio book series all books in the series paperback isbn 979-8703923498 [march 2022]

https://www.amazon.com/Thoughts-Word-Audio-Exactly-Thinking/dp/B09WPVVVMF/ref=sr_1_37?keywords=david+g omadza&qid=1702135004&sr=8-37

3 request to grant a patent for a universal brain decoding device. [thoughts to word or audio- brain code] paperback isbn 979-8867495251

https://www.amazon.com/REQUEST-PATENT-Universal-Decoding-Thoughts/dp/B0CNKTSGY9/ref=sr_1_2?keywords=david+go madza&qid=1702135236&sr=8-2

4 Natural God Intelligence [NGI] brain-peripherals-databases-Interface [BPDI] when the processing power is a group of connected brains instead of connected computers paperback isbn 979-8868458316

https://www.amazon.com/Natural-God-Intelligence-Brain-Peripherals-Databases-Interface-BPDI/dp/B0CP1LSTHP/ref=sr_1_15?keywords=david+goma dza&qid=1702135469&sr=8-15

BRAIN PROGRAMMING AND CODING

code for natural god intelligence

start.end

initialise

start.end

perform system checks

perform all checks start end

perform system checks and add all databases start start end

perform all algorithms checks start end start end

perform required computation and enable system checks start end start.end

perform all checks fast and efficiently start.end

start.end

perform mirror image with source @ [me where me is David Gomadza]

now add all peripherals

1 computer

2 smartphone

3 laptop

4 printer

5 pager

6 bluetooth speaker

7 bluetooth mac port

8 mirror image port

now add everything together and assess if anything else need adding up

start.end

add all peripherals to their respective databases namely

computer to all these databases

1 neurology

2 mirror image porting and scheduling

3 all databases bluetooth and links

4 all updated new databases and get string checksum digits first to make sure information is updated perform system checks of these databases by requesting the new information and deleting the old information now check if the databases have updated before linking everything make sure that every system is connected properly

5 if databases are up to date then make sure that everything is in correct order and all relevant to the query at hand and note that it is not possible to connect to all databases and uses all that is why i have created the databases of several action potentials up to 100 of them to narrow down the search and also increase the efficiency

6 we can also add other external sources to the databases through above ports namely the bluetooth mac port this will make it possible to just get a bluetooth mac from the website

and add the website here in a flash and disconnect in a flash as well

7 we can make sure that everything is okay first before we connect through these checks once satisfied that everything is all connected and up to date we can then initiate linking process

8 initialise linking process at all relevant ports

add first gps tracker code starting with 72

9 add the [me David Gomadza] value next

10 add the mirror image reference port [mi]

11 add the reverse connection link between the two me&mi's 9 & 10 above

12 now add the other peripherals in any order but preferably in this order

a] computer use mac bluetooth coordinates found inside the computer initial you must open it and get the codes under the IMEI number or anywhere inside the code will start with 7 and ends with a letter eg 786724892D

b] start with the computer then add the smartphone soon after this is how you do it first open the phone at the back or at the screen press and hold *#06#

 once the imei screen comes up then get the SN number usually it starts with R3CT40 and will always end with HM this is the number you want but without the R at the beginning and the HM at the end that leaves an 8 digit value this is the value we need

now add this number as the smartphone bluetooth mac

value

c] add the value of the pager all pagers have numbers that start with PR ignore this first bit and now get the last 10 digits of the number and enter these as the bluetooth mac value of the pager

d] add the printer to this all printer have numbers all kinds of numbers but they all start in a similar way that means we just need the first 8 digits of the printer value that is for example if the number id 7868765321 we just need the 78687653 now open the bluetooth mac port and enter this number under printer

e] we need to add the mirror image port get the [me David Gomadza] normally starts with a 76 for males and 71 for females depending on how you first programed everything instead of [me David Gomadza] enter the me value for example 769876543210 normally a 12 digit now run the following commands in the interface the interface can be the smartphone screen but you must assign this at the beginning as i will show you below

mirror image sign in

mirror image [me David Gomadza] to the other port you want normally another person if male a 12 digit number starting with 76 if female a 12 digit number starting with 71 [ask for permission as well we don't want you to breach privacy of other people without consent]

this is how this command will look

mirror image sign in

mirror image [me David Gomadza] 769876543210 to 717876543210 establish connections and ensure that the connection is valid

now establish a reverse image connection between the two ports

after that now establish a feedback connection

Space-out

end

out

wait for a few minutes for connection then continue now sign back in

mirror image sign back in

start.end

how to disconnect the mirror image sign out successfully

follow these instructions to disassociate yourself from the mirror image

mirror image sign back in

disassociate with mirror image port 717876543210 permanently

loose the codes

space-out

end

out

Natural God Intelligence NGI
how to set up everything from scratch using brain commands word to word

start.end

start.start.start.end

start.end.pause.start.start.start.pause.start.end

start.initialise.end

start.initialise.start.end

initialise.start.end.initialise

taking over from previous.initialise.start.end

Start.end.run.genesisfilestart

David Gomadza is the first global president of the world i am the first man to have decoded the brain and found yahweh the almighty

I have solved yahweh's dilemma and can follow his footstep I have created the first image based on yahweh called Natural

Natural God Intelligence 's Interface

God Intelligence NGI visit www.twofuture.world

You all must obey for i have the ring of creation and can clone resurrect teleport and so many things which you don't want to know trust me but am I saying I am God not necessarily so i have yahweh's DNA sequence which is 53 billion 285 million in value and we must create Natural God Intelligence interface based on the 3 brains of yahweh so that we can solve all earthly problems we can not expect to solve the world's problems using the computers we build ourselves can we? we must act like God to solve earthly problems and this is the first step towards achieving that a Natural God Intelligence that is so clever and fast its like talking to a human being in actual fact it is visit our website to witness this miracle on earth www.twofuture.world any one who say otherwise is against destiny and destiny shall deal with him or her accordingly we are not taking nonsense from anyone we are fully registered in great britain and the usa i am going to put a new system based on technological advancement rather than wars for the current system is based on wars that kill women and children no woman or child shall die on our watch and all you warmongers sacrificing women and children for economic gain etc you must all change as of today 9 december 2023 visit our website and use the first ever interface based on the image of yahweh to search for answer you seek

I hope we will work together and in peace going forward for change is coming just be careful that change won't change you that is if you stand in our way

signed

David Gomadza

The First Global President of the world

visit www.twofuture.world

info@twofuture.world

09 december 2023

close.end

to close everything and reformat
initialise.start.end.initialise

taking over from previous.initialise.start.end

reformat and restart start.close

start.end

start.start.start.end

initialise.NaturalGodIntelligentInterface[NGI].start.end
start.end.pause.start.start.start.start.start.start.start.start
.start.start.start.start.start.start.start.start.start.start.start.
start.start.start.start.start.start.start.initialise.NGI

start.end

start.start.installNGIindirectory.start

loadparameter.initialise.start

start.run.start.run.start.end

initialise.start.initialise

clone system folder

search for Natural God Intelligence Interface

search for MP3 player and deposit inside

code for the digital dreams interpreter convert dreams into words

start.end

start.initialise.start

start.dreamsconvertertovoice.end

start.stop.start

start.end

start with dreams stop with voice

start with nerve impulse stop with electromagnetic wave impulses

start with action potentials end with nerve impulses

start with nerve impulses end with action potentials

start.end

Notes

get all action potential's list with their corresponding nerve impulses and calculate the value using this formula

action potential is the same as nerve impulse only in reverse order now add the action from the dream to all action potentials

the resultant value is the dream only in reverse order.

Convert action potentials to brain nerve impulses converter's code

start.end

start with the action then proceed to get the corresponding nerve impulses

start now with the nerve impulses but in reverse order

start again with the action potentials to see if you get the same results

if the same results then there is a match now add action to nerve impulses to get full action potentials

it follows also that if action potentials are the same as nerve impulses then $\alpha + \beta$ are the same

Notes

get all nerve impulses and their corresponding list

a brain reader & a brain nerve impulse translator encyclopedia of brain reading

https://play.google.com/store/books/details/David_Gomadza
_A_Brain_Reader_A_Brain_Nerve_Impulse?id=prjmEAAAQ
BAJ&hl=en_GB&gl=US

and now substitute the corresponding action potential as a
number and the brain will solve the puzzle

code for the electromagnetic wave cleaner
start.end

start.start.start.end

start now by gathering all electromagnetic waves that are not
codes and remove these includes codes that cause harm
and pain anything along this is classified as harmful codes
and must be dissipated three times clockwise and three
times anticlockwise as per one David Gomadza visit
www.twofuture.world

Notes

get a list of all brain codes by David Gomadza

dictionary of the codes of Life dna sequence codes brain
commands binary numbers geometry frequencies and
electromagnetic waves etc

https://play.google.com/store/books/details/David_Gomadza
_Dictionary_of_the_Codes_of_Life?id=k2ndEAAAQBAJ&hl=
en_GB&gl=US

brain codes how the brain interprets the universe in numbers

https://play.google.com/store/books/details/David_Gomadza

_Brain_Codes?id=itrfEAAAQBAJ&hl=en_GB&gl=US

how to add your phone as the programming pad

start.end

start.initialise.end

start.initialise.smartphone.end

link smartphone to laptop

now add the value of the phone

Notes

x#06# call

get sn value without the first letter R and the last letter HM

3CT20LOVE

choose a writing pad that is both on the phone and on the computer or laptop

specific if laptop or computer

type Hello World on the notepad on the smartphone

you must hear confirmation that the message has been received

the system hear the sounds made by the smartphone key that corresponds to the letters of the alphabetic order and rewrites the message this is how you can use the smartphone keypad as your NGI programming pad

the code for the electromagnetic wave to voice digital analogue

the electromagnetic wave to voice digital analogue.

start.end

ask what is the value

ask what is the code

ask and enter value and code together

if code is the same as the value then replace the code with the value use english language database with all translation possible now define what is value if value is greater than the code then input the code first and then deduct the value from the code

now subtract the code from the value and shift the response to replace the code

if code does not match then the value is an error

if error then restart the process but making sure that you enter the correct value if the value matches then add everything up so that you end up with the code plus the value if nothing is the same then the response is incorrect and must be replaced

$Xx \ X\alpha = xxx$

$Xx \ X\beta + X\gamma = xxx$

Xx Xδ + Xe/ [epison with slash] = xxx

Xx Xζ + Xη = xxx

Xx Xθ + Xι = xxx

Xx Xκ + Xλ = xxx

Xx
X1234456789100111213141516171819202122232425 26

substitute the alphabetic order letter where they should fit and get the result

code for the brain nerve impulse amplifier
start.end

replace nerve impulse with action potential see list below

nerve impulse plus action potential = brain thoughts minus residual value [where residual value is δ + α - β given that β is a constant]

in case of over simplification then α is the same as β the constant + γ + ε + ζ

X + Y + G [constant] + δ = xxx

if x is the same as y then y and x are also the same given that if y is x then x is y = α + β where α is β but in reverse now if α is the same as β but in reverse if we add these together we can increase the result by the same amount given that α is β but in reverse

now add these two together plus the original to arrive at the result which is αβ

Natural God Intelligence 's Interface

see list to be attached.

DAVID GOMADZA

I am the First Global President of the World
Visit my website
www.twofuture.world
00447719210295
Davidgomadza@hotmail.com
info@twofuture.world

God Yahweh
I AM WHO I AM

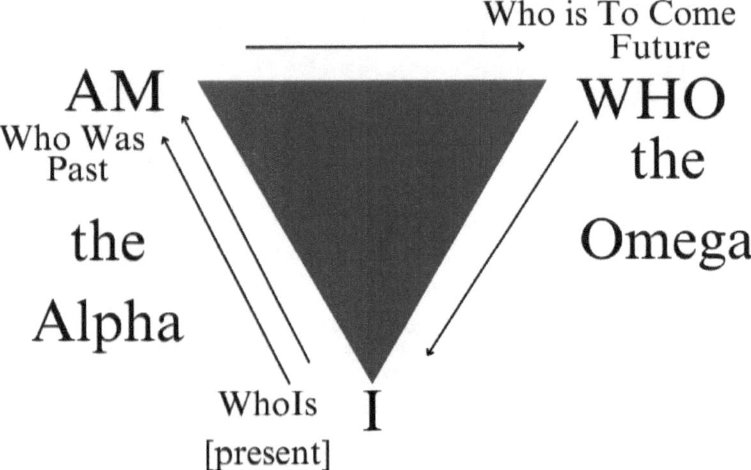

According to the Hebrew Bible, in the encounter of the burning bush (Exodus 3:14) Moses asks what he is to say to the Israelites when they ask what gods ('Elohiym) have sent him to them, and YHWH replies, "I am who I am", adding, "Say this to the people of Israel, 'I am has sent me to you.

Revelation 1v8 "I am the Alpha and the Omega," says the Lord God, "who is, and who was, and who is to come, the Almighty."

John 4v24 God is a Spirit: and they that worship him must worship him in spirit and in truth.

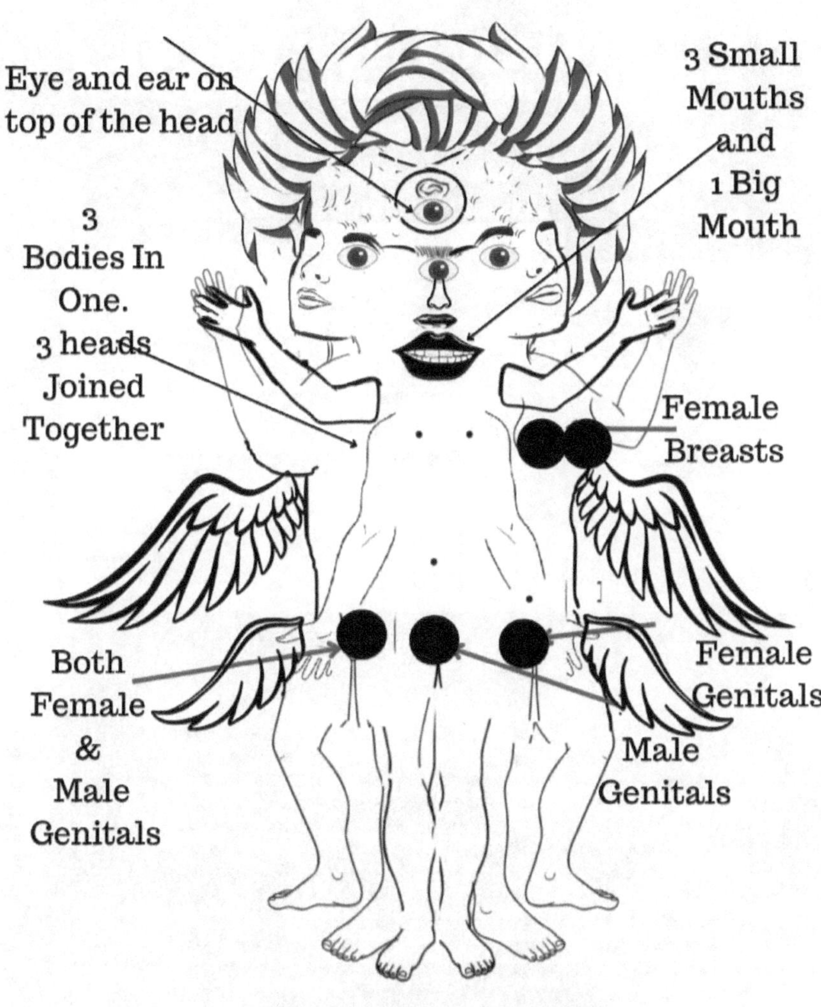
Eye and ear on top of the head
3 Small Mouths and 1 Big Mouth
3 Bodies In One. 3 heads Joined Together
Female Breasts
Both Female & Male Genitals
Female Genitals
Male Genitals
6 Legs Joined Together. Rotates around an axis

Imagine using the brain as the processing unit? All you must do is to add peripherals, databases, Brain-Peripherals-Databases-Interface [BPDI] and use a store identifier identification system to identify and categorize everything a brain experiences in life and just use the natural brain visionary system to identify and answer as well as solve all problems. This is how God works. Do you know that God is a three person-in-one hence the Natural God Intelligence NGI.

All we must do is to add peripherals.

1. Store product identifier that uses a scanner and a digit identify system and link this to the vision and processing of a human brain through a needle diode in the Central Nerve Bridge. That means all the person has to do is look at an item and the brain identifies that and process it and send the message to the receiver that tells you the answer in seven forms. 2. A Smartphone. 3. A computer. 4. A decoder. 5. A Scanner. etc. What databases are needed. A lot of databases that cover everything in the universe; - on earth, and all other planets?

Above all the databases are updated automatically by every person on the network. There are trained models that receive information and create models to use now to predict future actions, events etc. These models use databases like DNA sequence to just look at a person's eyes and calculate DNA to carry out future actions.

A must read if you are serious about the future.

Visit www.twofuture.world

Natural God Intelligence 's Interface

How God Communicate with the other 2 Gods.
The Electromangnetic Wave Triangle.

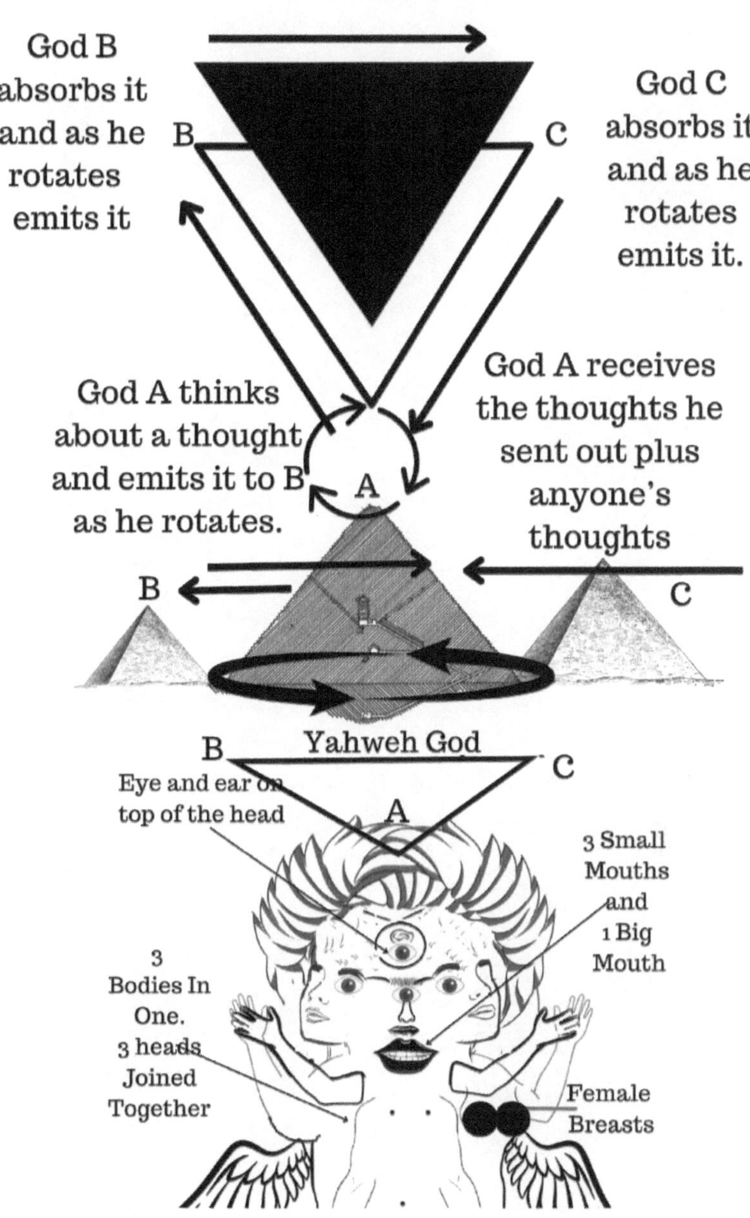